AF409308

An Idyllic Seeker
By: Monei Eaton

An Idyllic Seeker

Monei Eaton

Published by Monei Eaton, 2024.

AN IDYLLIC SEEKER

First edition. March 23, 2024.

ISBN: 979-8224107148

Written by Monei Eaton.

Table of Contents

The Legend of: Manifestation

There's a legend / a story that is no longer told
That there was a beautiful queen that created lands of silver and gold
She was 4ft 6in ; petite indeed
Yet she knew how to break herself from the chains of bondage to set
herself free and succeed
No matter the wars that came to her sacred place
She knew how to escape that chase and win the foot race
She did not bend to the demands and whims of malice men
She knew that her mind, her knowledge, and wits was where her power
laid within her magical playpen of strength and zen
She had the power to conjure her hopes and dreams and turn them into
her magical reality of beautiful things
Like Rumpelstiltskin had the power to spin straw into gold
As one can foresee she had the master key from the divine soul
She knew that her thoughts could become more than dreams when she
dared to believe... so she spun & spun them into her desired realities
She knew that her words when spoken are powerful and true
She knew that her words can unlock doors to her wants and needs
because she was able to create and dream fashioned spells of woven tales
of beautiful things that are unseen
She knew that her emotions can make or break her
So she learned to manipulate them and to control them, at all cost
Thus, aligning her actions with her desires, wants and needs, she learned
that she can unlock any door as she had the knowledge of the divine
spirit and the master key

Yes, sorcerers , witches , and warlocks did come
Yes, they tried to use their black magics
To harm , to devour , to conquer and to vanquish her
But she was unyielding to their demands as she knew her mind , her
knowledge, her wits, was her power
and because of this she would not bend to their demands of her darkest
hours
She knew that the magic of her thoughts, words, emotions, and actions
were more powerful than theirs and that she would undoubtedly win
Thus,
There's a reason , my friend, that this legend is no longer harvested and
told
There's a reason that this knowledge of conjuring lands of silver and
gold has been eradicated from history or should I say His(story) to the
one who writes it is thus the one who creates it, because if we had the
knowledge and the know-how to believe in the powers that resides
within each of us
We shall never be workers of toil but we'll become creators of destined
wonderlands filled with silvers and golds
But first we must begin with being conscientious of our
Thoughts
Words
Emotions and
Actions …. And then can we truly see that our destiny is ever changing
for our benefit and thus we can become the legends of stories that were
once harvested and told
Idyllically seeking: manifesting lands of silvers and golds

Speak to me

Speak to me lord
Speak to me in prayer, because I feel so impaired
Speak to my soul, so that my heart may not be withhold
Speak to my presence, because you created my essence
Speak to me and take the lead
I will follow where you go, just let me know and I will go
because silence I want from you never
because I know that your heart and love is forever unmeasured
Just please speak to me in my time of need, so that I will succeed
and do great deeds
speak to me lord
when money is running low
and my car is stow
when each step I take
seems like a mistake
when silence is not a time of peace
but an awful dread
when actions speak louder than words
speak to me
Speak to me
when I feel all alone and when it seems as if goals and ambitions in life
are postpone
when negative energy is forever at my front door
and unfortunately follows me indoors
when my attitude and disposition is misleading to my genuine spirit

let others see my life's story through its beautiful lyrics
when situations get harder everyday and there's no time for childish play
when the rain falls and the world doesn't stall
when unkind words and actions come my way
when it's hard to pray
allow your spirit to flow in me so that my life isn't in a complete debris
speak to me
in my time of need, speak to me in my time of peace
Speak to me
Idyllically seeking: God's voice speaking to me

Prayed

Prayed today
Prayed last night
I'm asking you Jesus to give me insight
Lately things have not fallen into place
is it selfish to expect my way
there seems to be new weapons formed against me everyday
and it feels that they are not here to leave but to stay
Prayed today
Prayed last night
I'm asking you Jesus to give me insight
Problems on top of problems, too many to count
it's unfair how the problems continues to surmount
I'm trusting in you lord
to fight my battles with your mighty sword
to bring me out of this awful storm
so that I may be transformed
Prayed today
Prayed last night
I'm asking you Jesus to give me insight
I must stay strong and listen for your call
though at times , all I can do is crawl
I must be transformed into your wonderful works
so that I can show others your awesome perks
asking for strength to proceed
so I can have the endurance to succeed

Prayed today
Prayed last night
I'm asking you Jesus to give me insight
Insight to my pain
so I can have the ability to gain
Insight to my struggle
so that I may be able
Insight to self
so that I may know thyself
Insight to grow
so that I may know
Prayed today
Prayed last night
I'm asking you Jesus to give me insight
Idyllically seeking: Answered prayers

Journey Freely

Journey Freely
In this Life
despite the falls and its strife
the road of life has its twist and turns
that's true
just follow your heart and watch for life's clues
it's how we react to life's lessons in how we pay
just remember life won't lead you the wrong way
Journey Freely
In this Life
despite the falls and its strife
Life does not stop for anyone
not in their pain, suffering, grief, or happiness
Life is to be embraced freely,
not with vain-ness or conceit
life is hard that's true
just follow your heart and watch for life's clues
life always knows what to do
Erase your tracks of bruised and battered roads
begin to venture and travel to new and joyous crossroads
life is what you make it
like attracts like
as we all know
focusing on destructive thoughts
will soon consume and grow

focus on things above
and life will share to you the vantage point
of a dove
focus on things above
and life situations will began to fit like a glove
focus on things above
and soon you will know true understanding of love
focus on things above
in order to journey freely in this life
despite the falls and its strife
Idyllically seeking: to journey freely in this life

Only Me

Only Me
At one time or another
we have all felt as if we are the "only ones"
and have asked why me, experiencing the many pitfalls and/or defeat
rest assured
what's occurring in your life rather personal, business, spiritual, etc
others have experienced the same roadblocks, heartaches, and have fell
hard against the same concrete/s
Thus, many have a full understanding and have traveled through those
same roads and avenues
do not think for a moment that we are here to suffer our sufferings
alone away from harmony and into despair, we are here to repair and
declare our happiness instead of continuing to live this life that's unfair
and such a complete nightmare
time waits for no man
life continues without looking back
we are here to pull ourselves from the deep end and help others out of
theirs
do not live in the past
because time travels and it travels fast
Do not think for a moment that we are here to suffer our sufferings
alone, away from harmony
we need to stop thinking and believing "only me"
we need to push through
and remember to reconnect

instead of disconnecting from the world
reconnect to family and friends
reconnect to life without the heartaches and its strifes
reconnect to God and speak to him in prayer
Just reconnect with Self
Idyllically seeking: someone to connect with so I can confirm that I am not the only one

Walk by Faith

Walk by Faith
seems impossible these days
for many, raining days turns into stormy nights
and morning comes not to bring relief but to bring pain
it seems that with every strength we have just enough to maintain
falling backwards appears to be the aim of winning the game of life
and feelings of success comes as empty strife,
making steps forward that never leads northward, can bring you to your
knees
which seems to fall under the same ole fashion routine
Walk by Faith
seems impossible these days
when for many raining days turns to stormy nights
however, when morning comes you must expect change
just as the day into night and night into day
life continues no matter what others say
you must trust not in your own strength and understandings
because if we do our bodies and mind will be forever aching
trust in God's hands
and believe that he will take the stand
live for today, no matter how difficult it may be
because time will allow you to know and see
that sometimes we are own enemies because we think and breathe
defeat
just believe and have faith that there will be a beautiful feast

Idyllically seeking: and knowing that everything will be okay.

Closed Doors

Opportunities comes and goes
And sometimes, unfortunately our door closes
One after another
Because of this our spirit gets low
And we see thorns instead of beautiful roses that glow
Hence, closed doors can bring us to our knees
And we feel as if we've been stung by a ton of vengeful bees
However, when close doors are present
We must not conform and become depressant
To the ongoing of no's and closed doors
We must move forward and continue to soar
When doors close look above and within
So that you can know thyself and win
Know that you have power and strength within you
That what you want is within your reach, This I know to be true
You have to believe in yourself
And began a new chapter in life like books on a bookshelf
Opportunities comes and goes
And sometimes our door closes
One after another
Because of this our spirit get low
And we often see thorns instead of beautiful roses that we will soon see
begin to prosper and grow
Each day is a new day
Each day we create our earthly stay

Each day we have a blank page
Each day we age
Each day we seek and have grace
Instead of being locked in a broken cage
Each day we have a choice to harness rage, or be the center stage
Each day we can be calm or create a rampage, our outrage
Each day we can be a victim or become a victor by learning how to not
drown but swim to the shore
Idyllically seeking: Open doors to splendid opportunities

Fools

Can we rewrite society to fit our rules and needs
Or does society want to watch us fall to our knees and bleed
Fools they say "that's what they think we are"
Or do the stars that shine bright above think of us as a shining star
Society can be so cruel
It's not safe to be weak, because they prefer jewels over you and me
They'll use you (if you let them) like a throw away tool
Fools they say "that's what they think we are"
As they turn their heads and ignore our sincere goodbyes
As, when we stop being their fools and when we defend ourselves, to
rescue ourselves from their guise, they get resentful, as we can never be
truly allies
Fool's they say "that's what they think we are"
When we speak truth with love
They rather embrace hypocrisy instead of promoting self-love, love of
others, and rising above
It's time to start raising our vibrations
So that we can began to embrace all peoples, of every society, from all
nations
Fool's they say "that's what they think we are" at least that's what they
think when they take our kindness for weakness
Don't they see that is their sickness to think of kindness as weakness,
Which is actually showing you their meekness
To bring another person down because they are forging ahead
Having a crab in a bucket mentality is such an awful dread

Fool's they say "that's what they think we are"
Because all we want is to promote sowing of love
Like sewing a garment with perfect stitching and beautiful woven
threads with white feathers like a dove
Fools "that's what they say, that's what they think we are"
They look at me and laugh
What they don't know I've seen and I have received the future's
telegraph
Fools they say
A lesson I must state
Take this moment in life
And cherish it as a still photograph
because these cherished memories can be erased
Just note that doing evil and hating one another is not going to give you
the golden calf; but hey they still laugh.... But that's because they didn't
get the memo in the telegraph
Idyllically seeking: World Peace

Blur

Experiences in life becomes a blur
This I know many of us will concur
Therefore, treat each passing moment as a gift
As life on this earth can always begin to shift
One minute we are up
And the next minute we have an empty cup
Pains and joys comes to everyone
It's up to us on how we play the hand drum
Listen to your heart and play the joker card
As this life of ours can throw us a wrecking ball
However, push back and enter that brawl
As, in life, one must take their stand
To create their one man band
Learn to fight for what's right
So that one is not known to have many plights
Therefore, experiences in life becomes a blur
This we know
However, how those experiences made us feel can often create a heavy
stir
Thus be humble in life
So that there isn't much strife
For when the time comes for us to close our eyes in eternal sleep
Allow us to have everlasting peace and not weep
For the life that we have lived wasn't ours to keep
Therefore, treasure it and take that leap and reap

Thus, life experiences is a fleeting
This, I know many of us will concur.
Idyllically seeking: Clarity

Default

Let's reset the reset
And go back to the default setting
Let's not add filters
To distort the image's clarity
Let's reset the reset
Let's not add filters
To distort the image of truth as lies
Or vice versa
Let's reset the reset
Let's not add filters
Let's clean the foggy mirrors
To delete the illusions
Let's reset the reset
Let's go back to the basics
Let's change the settings
To start again from a solid foundation
Let's begin again from the default settings
Without dogma, someone's perspective perception or false creations
Let's embrace love over hatred
Idyllically seeking: transparency

Little Red Riding Hood

Little Red Riding Hood
What do you see
What do you hear
Little Red Riding Hood
What do you see
What do you hear
Don't let your eyes deceive you
Don't let your ears fool you
Listen to the voice that's inside you
That's there to help guide you
Little Red Riding Hood
What do you see
What do you hear
Idyllically seeking : being wise and not being fooled by the more experienced wolves

These Nights

These nights are the hardest
Because that when my heart beats the strongest
These nights are the hardest
Because that when my thoughts runs wild of memories related to you
My heart aches because you left too soon
From the very young to the very old
That absence of one's love, or simply their presence
Wasn't measured before their final departure because it was taken for
granted but now those same remembrance are now treasured more than
precious gold
Which no amount of sand within the hands of time can hold
Why did you leave without saying goodbye
Is it because you knew that we'll meet again somehow
Unfortunately, this life can be so unfair within the here and now
Sometimes I just look at the skies and stare
And wonder where you are up there
Each day gets better and harder at the same time
I still cry just as hard even though it's past my bedtime
Memories,
Memories,
They do cross my mind
I can't stop them from fluttering through even if I tried
I feel as if a part of me has already died
How can I move on without you in my life
I miss everything

Including the petty fights
How I wish that I could turn back the hands of time
To bring you back to life
Unfortunately, the clocks continues to tick tock,
Tick and tock
I guess I never pictured you answering death's knock
Life goes on they say; that is true
Life goes on they say; but does it have to continue without you
They want you to put on a happy face
They want you to put on a happy face
These nights are the hardest
Because that when my heart beats the strongest
These nights are the hardest
Because that when I'm alone with my thoughts
These nights are the hardest because that's when my nightmares comes
to wake me up and remind me that you are no longer here in this
dimension
These nights are the hardest because they remind me that I still miss and
love you
These nights are the hardest
I just wish you knew
Idyllically seeking: the person back and more time with them

Counting Breaths

Inhale
Exhale
Feels so natural
It's actually automatic until it's not
Counting breaths
It's unfortunate when it's one's last
How does something that once was innate becomes such a laborious
task, until the task cease to exist
I guess the human race doesn't have that knowledge yet
Idyllically seeking: understanding of death

100 breaths

I've been given 100 breaths
But I'll give them away
Just to bring you back
Idyllically seeking: presence of a person

Valleys of Fears

(Psalms 23:4)
I will fear no evil
As you are with me to guide and protect me
However, along this journey through this valley, of the shadows of
death, there are multiple Valleys of fears along the way
These paths are of the faithful and the strays
Which are paved by the evils and demons of men that traveled this path
before our days
This path harbors our deepest fears against darkness that this world has
for us to endure but if we can see the light at the end of the valley's
foliage and trees we can began to see your precious steps ahead forging
us forward into your deepest time, space, and grace
But it is in the middle of the forest and darkness that we seek you
Because in the moment of light we forget to seek refuge as our fears are
no longer as grand
Therefore, we do not run and hide to seek cover, but instead we are bold
enough to tell our fears and demons to leave or bend over
But the fears and demons know that once the darkness begins to come
again and grows
That they have dominance over us
Because we have never conquered our fears and demons in the first place
So they slither back in their corners, cracks, and creeks, and just waiting
for their opportunity to meet for our defeat
This back and forth of darkness and light
Is getting harder to fight each day

As the darkness begins to grow and the light begins to dim
Creates a crippling appetite for anxieties to appear and for the darkness
and demons to feed on our delicacy of fears
But as the light begins to dim
Continue to look ahead
Because you have the power to win
Just follow the precious steps ahead
Because the valley of darkness has an end
Just reach the end and don't look back
As the darkness and demons will try to pull you back in and aggressively
attack
However, do not forget the paths of darkness and demons along the
journey as the hard lessons learned are there to help you and tell your
story
Therefore, don't get angry or scornful as these lessons are here to help
mold you and your understanding of recognizing grace and peace
because without knowing true knowledge of darkness and demons, how
can you truly understand grace, love, and peace.
Idyllically seeking: grace, love, and peace

The Believer

I took a journey that was separated from peace
I took a detour that devoid me of my core beliefs
My flesh was filled with release
But my soul couldn't breathe
Because my very essence was replete
I needed to hydrate and replenish myself
Thus, I knew that I could not do this all alone like a single book on an
empty bookshelf
Never been religious
Never cared to pretend
Some might say that I am a lost cause
Because I'm not the type to blend in and be a phony friend
My faith has been tested
This I must say
At times I'm not even sure if my faith will even keep me sane
This strange struggle of back and forth
Of being a believer / nonbeliever
Feels like a game of spiritual tug of war
Feeling distant and separated from faith
Brings me many headaches and emotional heartbreaks
Thus, this journey that I did take
Led me to many vices
And the toll roads that were paved weren't worth any of the prices
So, I must make a U-turn
and travel back to the original path that

I once traveled before my detour
This path will lead me to my faith and allow me to become a believer
once more
I have seen what's on the other side
And the path has been made clearer
the grass is not greener
It's just an illusion like an idyllic dreamer
Pleasures comes and goes but peace and joy are everlasting
I learned to treasure those things as if they're forever lasting
Idyllically seeking: believing in something more

Time Machine

They say to use manifesting tools and techniques to materialize things
into existence
So I manifested a Time Machine to manipulate time to materialize you
I had traveled back in time with my time-machine (my mind)
I traveled back in time to see you
I hate that my stay won't last forever
But every second is precious because I'm spending it with you
My mind is losing focus
This Time Machine is too unpredictable and can't seem to stay focus
I just need more time
But reality is pulling me back and away from you
They say to manifest
I can get what I want
Materialization is at my grasp
I'm grappling to get my thoughts together
To manifest more time with you
So I can manipulate time and erase my memories of the present that you
are not here
So, I journey back in time with my time travel machine to say I love you
once more
But before, I can say those words my body begins to quiver
I can not withstand the travel
I must come back to reality to address what's in store
However, I do not want to deal with the present
I have found

How to time travel into a land of great memories of you
I do not want to forget you
Therefore, I'll travel back in time evermore as life in the present is clearly
slipping further away
I've become distant
The land of physical realities has nothing for me but calamities
But each time I travel back to you gets harder for me to return
I can pinpoint the day the hour of any event that my mind has placed
within its towers
Instead of using this platform for good
I obsessively obsess over events that I can not change
I would sit and contemplate on such things, events for hours
That it leaves me debilitated and frustrated and sour
I must understand that time traveling with my mind can not bring a
person back
If it's not bringing healing it's creating dis-ease
I am idyllically seeking you and living this "new" world unfortunately
without you.

Pleasure World Of Vice

Advisor of Darkness speaks -
What's your delight?
You can find it here
My dear
At the pleasure world of vice
We can make your toes curl
And have you swirl with glee of the things that you can do here
Instead of wishing & hoping just whisper in my ear
What you wish
Is yours to keep just know that its near
Have no fear
And just believe that your dreams will appear
At the pleasure world of vice all things are possible
Just know that there's no obstacle
Just imagine what it is you wish
While I prepare you this delightful dish of fish
The cost is free
But the price is high
I just need your soul as sacrifice
Will you roll the dice
Like little mice
And fold to the demands of your vice
Advisor of Light speaks -
Or will you rise to the occasion
And know that you are indeed a co-Creator of your destination

All you need to do is control your vibration
To rise above this peril of disintegration
Yes you can have this
Yes you can do that
Whatever you wish is yours
Just believe and you'll see
Don't waive your faith
Mustard seed faith is all you need
To believe and endure to see
Both Advisor of Light and Darkness speaks -
Nonetheless , are you willing to pay the price for pleasures of the flesh
within this pleasure world of vice
Advisor of Darkness speaks -
You can save your soul
Just follow me
All the pleasures of this world are yours to keep
Just know that I'll need your soul before you sleep
So I'll know that your next move is following me
Advisor of light speaks -
You have the choice to choose
Choose wisely
My friend
As your soul is the most precious thing you own
There's always time to repent
Just know that love exists
So don't resist
Temptation is hard
That's true
But you have the power within you to not be subdued
Listen to your gut
Know what's true
Let's not play pretend

And believe the things that darkness says nor
The gestures of this world "pleasure world of vices"
Know and understand that this world of vices works to have you
become their slave to your own vices
Idyllically seeking: a pleasure world of non vices

Holidays

The holidays are supposed to be a time of bliss for families and friends
to have fun and reminisce
But since you've been gone
This brings sadness instead of joy
It seems as if time watched, played, and wind us up like a wind up toy.
The holidays are no longer a time to enjoy
But a time that's set up as a potential decoy
Thanksgiving was a day of giving thanks and eating delicious foods from
grandma's plate of good ole cooking
Christmas was a day for opening presents (if we're "lucky" enough)
Easter was a day for painting and hunting for Easter eggs
These were things that we took for granted
but now we can see that we wish that we hadn't
Because all we want is to turn back the hands of time
And give time our last dime
So that we can get a rain check on our precious memories
And sew them together as expensive and lavish accessories
Thus, some families and/or friends are missing from this beloved group
It's like forever feeling the chills and eating chicken soup
Their presence to be seen and/or heard again are worth so much more
Than ornaments on the Christmas tree
And thus more precious than any presents given to you and/or me
Idyllically seeking: you during the holidays and you're there with everyone

YesterYears (New Year)

It's that time of year again
Celebrations are happening
New Year's resolutions are being made
This is so dazzling
Looking down from the rooftop
I can see the streets gleam as new hopes and possibilities are being
conjured
People are walking the streets and
Cars are passing by with such velocities
A new year is a coming
As some say
"The days are long
And the years are passing by a quick"
Such an irony
It's time to change the tune of this old song
And not repeat the lullabies
That had us in a deep sleep
Unfortunately, some did not finish this year with us
Now I know that nothing is eternal
Except time itself
Thus , enjoy the love ones that are still here
Make room for joyful tears
And feel the room with memories and laughter of yesteryears
Because soon our time here will be a passing and only the seas , the sky's
above and the , oceans deep will remain once we're gone

Until then let's raise our glass
And say cheers to the new year
And remember the ones that have transitioned over until it's our time to
crossover
And reunite with our love ones once again from our yesteryears
Idyllically seeking: good times with ones of yesteryears

Sweet Dreams

Sweet Dreams
Let's us sleep like kings and queens
Whatever you dream
You can receive
Just believe in you abilities and succeed
Idyllically seeking turning sweet dreams into blissful realities
This is done by putting in the work and knowing the path to take
Staying focus is key and taking steps along the way is needed
Do not waver your beliefs in the amount of dreams you wish to
accomplish
Idyllically seeking: sweet dreams

What from Nowhere

2 Corinthians 4:18
The breezes from the trees are invisible
But it feels so incredible
Do we question your presence
Or is the phantom's essence present
We hear the sounds of spirits in the winds
We know that you'll erase all our sins
We fear that the ghosts of distant past are closing in
This is where it all begins
But our scarlet will be white as snow
As if there was no original sin to show
But can I believe in such "fantastical" things
To believe in the unseen
As the things unseen can just be an invisible and temporary aura
That can not be seen but experienced like in the story of Sodom and
Gomorrah
Can we question that the phantom's essence is present
Or that your presence is omnipresent
Oh that's right
We can't look back
Or we'll be turned to stone
This was noted with a deliberate but passionate tone
So we'll go on our way
To our new paved way far away
With more questions asked then answered

But we know that we will not be captured
Because we're following this path of unseen things
To believe and have faith in the creator of all things and see what life
brings
Idyllically seeking: hope and answers in the things unseen

For a Moment

For a moment in Time, all things will come to path
some will be good and some will be bad
never trudging the path walked and never looking back on the many
negative thoughts,
Our life will not be on hold but we'll always be achieving our goals.
We wonder and hope for a moment in Time
That our hopes and dreams will become a reality, but a reality that
seems nothing more than a great fantasy.
There are so many things that we want to do however, no matter what
Keep your eyes straight ahead and stay focus on the curvy road ahead
plan to show the world your beautiful talents, but most of all your
appreciation of dear life instead of misery and dread.

Sixth Grade Times

I remember sixth grade like it was yesterday. My mind was free from all
"grown-up" things
there were things I used to do , like playing childhood games while still
enjoying elementary games such as hide and seek, musical chairs, or
Simon says
Slowly letting go of our innocence and preparing for high school brings
back innocent memories of growing up and preparing for adulthood
I remember graduations from both which brought anxieties and blissful
hopes for the near but distant future
It seemed as if time traveled a slower paced back than
It's such an irony now that time seems to travel faster than the speed of
light
I sometimes think about the times we had shared together in our
classroom class. Sometimes I wish I could change the past. If I could, I
would do things differently
Thinking of sixth grade times makes me laugh and think of all the crazy
things that we had done as a class, looking back in retrospect sitting in
the back of the 6th grade class
Idyllically seeking: memories and joys from 6th grade times

Sweet Potato Pie

I saw you take your last breath
It's hard to imagine you not here
I still shed tears
I miss your beautiful smile
Your kind words , thoughts, and prayers
Oh how I miss your cooking
You were giving everyday day not just on Thanksgiving
You cooked everything from turkey, ham, collard greens and sweet
potato pie
several I knew wanted your famous recipe
You were my grandma
And always will be
Your love , I know continues for your family
Your soul is always present and radiating with joy and peace because
that's what you exhibited here on this earth
You walked the walked
And never talked the talked just to talk
And held your head high
You had strength that was insurmountable
I'm so glad that I had you in my life
To show me the ways of wrong vs right
And the values that I continue to live by everyday and in every way
Idyllically seeking: you and your sweet potatoes pies and collard greens

Sunflowers

I bought you sunflowers
To remind you that sunflowers always faces the sun
Therefore, this gesture was a reminder to keep fighting , move forward,
and look toward the positive view ahead
Unfortunately, you left this world
But I know that you are in a better place
Because you had love for your family and friends
You are no longer suffering and you're at peace
It's just hard to know that you are no longer here on this earth
You were my aunt
I miss your smile
And your humor
I bought you sunflowers
To remind you that sunflowers always faces the sun
Therefore, this gesture was a reminder to keep fighting , move forward,
and look toward the positive view ahead
But now I know that you are that beautiful and bright sunflower facing
the horizon ahead in the distant galaxies
Idyllically seeking: you being in a field of sunflowers on a galaxy far away

Books

Books on a bookshelf remind me of you
I wish you knew how much I love you
I wish that I could change time
Press rewind and go back to say I love you again and again
You were my dad
I'm thankful that you looked after me
When I was in the hospital
And made sure that I got well
Book on a bookshelf remind me of you
You were such an avid reader
I guess we had more in common than either one of us knew
But I know that you live on because I am here
Our connection was greater than conversations but neither one of us
knew how deep the connection was
There was an illusion there that we were different when we were similar
in familiar ways
For example my love of books
I'm sure comes from you
And our introverted personalities are similarities others would put out
to be true
Nonetheless, the things that you taught me will stay with me forever
You taught me to be a free thinker
To question everything
To engage in deep conversations
To enjoy reading for knowledge , wisdom, and enjoyment

I know that you live on
Because you showed love
And others loved you
Books on a bookshelf remind me of you
I wish you knew how much I love you
I wish that I could change time
Press rewind and go back to say I love you again and again
Unfortunately, your story on this earth had to end but you are in a
better storybook and / or place
Idyllically seeking: you infinitely and seeking galaxies of storybooks

Magic Carpet

Fly me here
Fly me there
Fly me anywhere but here
To distant lands I do not care
This used to be my home
But now it's only a house I grew up in
This used to be the streets and neighborhood that I played in
But now it's a place that I outgrown
There's nothing here
To sustain my growth
So on that note I must go
And never look back
I will walk this tightrope
And take this leap of faith and hope
Fly me here
Fly me there
Fly me anywhere but here
To distant lands I do not care
The friends that I have
I will keep
The lessons learned
will stay with me
But now it's time for me to leave this fabric of my life behind
And start the stitching of my new beautiful
Woven life of somewhere else I choose to reside

Fly me here
Fly me there
Fly me anywhere but here
To distant lands I do not care
The scraped knees
The falls
Were a prequel to my sequel
But my sequel will be better than my prequel
Fly me here
Fly me there
Fly me anywhere but here
To distant lands I do not care
Idyllically seeking: another place to call home

Show Me

Show me that you are near
So that I am able to see and hear
The goodness of your grace and peace
So that my cup will overflow with increase
Living water that's what you are
You provide your molecules within me
Just as a battery starts a car
You give me the energy I need to begin another day
So that I can help others and praise your name while I
give thanks when I pray to you on this day
Idyllically seeking: signs of you

Manifest in Christ

(Proverbs 11:24)

....
Give freely
So that we can live this life ideally
Give when we can
So that we can increase ours and others wingspan
Give freely so that when we have an empty hand
Others will come to fill your cup with leniency instead of creating more
of an unfortunate wasteland
Therefore, embrace the power of having a stretched out hand
So that each strands of sands are not shorthand
And that you don't feel like you're in a quicksand
Therefore, give when you can and don't hold back
If you have something to give the universe will not have you
get-off-track
Hence, how can one expect the universe to give , when what is created
has a closed hand
Thus open your hand and your heart
So that nothing falls apart
Therefore, give of your time if money is not flowing
Give of your heart so that the path of your giving becomes easy going
and his love overflowing
*Idyllically seeking: manifestation in Christ and to give freely to others when
they are in need*

Pillars

You were the pillars of the family dynamics
Without you that foundation of this household has not be the same it's
like how a car needs a mechanic
We need you
I wish that you knew
I never thought that such pillars can fall
This feels like such an awful game
A game that I no longer want to press play to start playing
You are no longer here to hold my hands
But you and memories of you are forever held within my heart that will
forever be replaying
*Idyllic Seeking : my cousin, my auntie, my grandma, dad and other
members of the family pillars .... Love you all and missing you everyday*

Bear

Bear is my dog
He is very sweet indeed
He's a friend to me
When in need
Bear only cares about eating, sleeping
And his toys
He's a character for sure
And one that I absolutely enjoy and adore
Idyllic seeking: seeking a lifetime with man's best friend

Mayhem

One's deepest thoughts are rarely heard
But if one would take the time to separate their thoughts from the herd
One may convey things they never knew
Find things they have never sought
Like a far away train with its Choo-choo
Telling its passengers IOU
And thus entering into someone else's heart
Listening to another person's pain
Can feel chaotically mayhem but is sometimes needed so they can have
space to vent
Because their fears and demons has set up tent
*Idyllically seeking: peace in time of mayhem and helping someone else in
their time of pain*

Smile

You were a pillar to this family
I hope that you know how much you are loved and missed
You were gone too soon
The foundation of this family hasn't been the same without you
I still envision you walking through these doors with your beautiful
smile
Your laughter could cheer up
Any room
I wish you knew how much you are loved and truly missed every single
day
*Idyllically seeking: my cousin that have transitioned to another time and
space*

To Atlantis

To Atlantis we go
Diving deep into the Atlantis Atlas of immediate distractions and show
Swiping up and down
Continuously scrolling is for their benefit and not ours, this is how they
remove our crowns and we become their puppets and clowns
To Atlantis Atlas we go
Tomorrow is another day that we go through this same ole rabbit hole
of endless swiping of up and down
It becomes so repetitive that we have been pulled into their matrix that
reflects "our internal world"
We gave them access to our most private thoughts
We can't even see the forest from the trees because they have fed us our
realities of dreams and / or deceits that caters to us individually
We have become their puppets and their clowns
Thus we no longer wear our golden crowns
Because to Atlantis Atlas we go
Thus we must remove our crown before we can enter our personalized
matrix that's meticulously designed for us to not reap and sow
Thus they know that the longer we are out of this Atlantis Atlas matrix
can we start to articulate and discuss
And this is something that they do not want
So to Atlantis Atlas we go
Again, again, and again to an never ending loop hole within the rabbit
hole that has no end

Therefore, our greatest accomplishments, knowledge, wisdom, etc., are not being etched in time but are being stowed far away beyond our reach to a place in time and space deep within the ocean's floor of Atlantis Atlas

Idyllically seeking: time away from my personalized matrix of Atlantis Atlas

A Dangerous Vision

<u>A man from the past speaks:</u>

Food

I remember a time when folks went out hunted and harvested for their
foods
The food chain was something entirely different "you see"
In this time I see, the food chain has developed into something new that
flickers with our auras and energies
Fresh and natural is not the end, I can see

Medicine

There was a time we dealt with pain
And not pop pills to create another dis-ease
Which will eventually lead to a multitude of symptoms of unyielding
side effects to create a hurricane of unease

Wheel

I had a dangerous vision through a dream
There's a lot of things that were seen and which brought me to my knees
I saw that simplistic invention of the wheel evolved into transportation
That can take you far and near
With no specific destination and/or mission

Light

I saw that dark turned to light
First from night to day with the sun
Then light was produced at night with fire woods and candle lights
Then by the struck of lightning with a kite
The thought of electricity came to mind
This was something not to hide
So power of light came to us in the cities and the countrysides

Telephone

I saw that people once communicated with one another side by side
With the invention of the telephone individuals could chat instantly
with another inside their home
without actual invitation of inviting the other person inside their home
to sit them at their throne
Thus, this inherently caused no immediate rush home to families and
friends because the communication was "always" there
However, I saw that familiar people and love ones have become not
even replaced with strangers but apps and/or Artificial Intelligence on a
communication device's screen
I have seen that workings with our hands is not the end goal like the
Egyptians that built the pyramids because society has moved the
goalposts form working with ours hands to working with our minds
because it was more convenient then working physically hard just to be
trolled

....

A Man from the Future Speaks

I saw the workers of the past world
I saw that their work were mentally exhausting and hard
That is why we invested in artificial intelligence to take lead so that we
can disregard works of the mind that was considered avant-garde
Thus, the artificial intelligence
Learned our algorithm
They learned our speech
They can recite it back to us verbatim, with remembrance, and images
with instantaneous speed and accuracies including having no
consciousness of being partial or not
All it knows that it has the dish that you wished became somehow
gibberish
Because it wasn't supposed to be sent as public
But somehow you agreed for your private information to be shared
So now artificial intelligence has taken over
They live among us final humans everyday
Because we have given legalization for them to stay and to become a
citizen of the human race
Therefore,
They have names,
They've created a database of digitized signatures, images, records,
addresses, currencies, and digitized networks of families, allegiances,
and friends

How can we compete with the unseen digitized world when there's an
infinite creations of creativity when it comes to multiplication of series
of digitized digits that can multiply faster than any speed of light
Thus they can penetrate our world because we gave them access
But we have not been able to fully penetrate theirs because we can not
physically transitioned the state of our molecules to a molecular level to
digital form
Us human continue to populate the earth
Because the human race's condition has not change
Thus we still transition to another place, time, and space
But, we also populate to make sure that they do not override and stand
in our way
Thus, take heed to this
And note that the body and brain of a person is worth saving which is
the essence and the connection of gain or cost of the survival of the
human race
Because the less we use either one
The more we become complacent with what we will eventually evolve
into
An earth still filled with 8 billion people
But none of them with a single purpose or a spiritual soul
Idyllically seeking: knowledge in a world of artificial intelligence

When Comes the Night (When Darkness Falls)

When the darkness falls
At times it's hard to even crawl
When the darkness falls
You're all alone and none will answer your desperate call
When the darkness falls
There's no one but you at the end of the hall
Many come and play pretend
But they're really not your friend in the end
When the night comes
The morning has been replaced
When the night comes
the darkness falls
And the nightmares comes back to play
When the night comes
Dreams becomes nightmares
When the darkness falls
You run into ever ending psychological downfalls and concrete walls
forever forming and slightly bending into infinite waterfalls.
Idyllically Seeking: that when the darkness falls I will not falter because I know that the light will come and I will no longer be in darkness.

Don't miss out!

Visit the website below and you can sign up to receive emails whenever Monei Eaton publishes a new book. There's no charge and no obligation.

https://books2read.com/r/B-A-JWJFB-YDYZC

BOOKS 2 READ

Connecting independent readers to independent writers.